Texas A&M Aggies IQ: The Ultimate Test of True Fandom

Walter B. Littlejohn

Printed in the United States of America

IQ Series books are the trademark of Black Mesa Publishing, LLC.

Cataloging-in-Publication Data is available from the Library of Congress.

ISBN: 978-0-9837922-3-9
First edition, first printing

Cover photo courtesy of Kelly J. Russo, Class of '95.

Black Mesa Publishing, LLC
Florida
David Horne and Marc CB Maxwell
Black.Mesa.Publishing@gmail.com

Texas A&M Aggies Football

Contents

"Played wholeheartedly, football is a soul-satisfying outlet for the rugged, courageous type of boy who likes physical contact. Played halfheartedly, football is a waste of time and energy. Football is no halfway game."
— D.X. Bible

Introduction

WHAT'S IT LIKE to be an Aggie? If you are one, you can't explain it. If you're not one you can't understand it. Texas A&M played its first football game in 1894. It is a program so steeped in tradition that it's sometimes hard to tell fact from fiction.

But, there's no fiction here.

It's all facts.

Gig 'em Aggies.

Texas A&M Aggies IQ

Chapter 1

The Fighting Texas Aggies

WORDS FROM THE Texas A&M school song tell it better than anything else ...

> We are the Aggies - the Aggies are we
> True to each other as Aggies can be
> We've got to FIGHT boys
> We've got to fight!
> We've got to fight for Maroon and White
> After they've boosted all the rest
> They will come and join the best
> For we are the Aggies - the Aggies are we
> We're from Texas A.M.C.

No school has its traditions more interwoven with daily student life than Texas A&M. This is no better illustrated than in the Aggies renowned 12th Man tradition. The tradition began in the 1922 Dixie Classic, the forerunner of the Cotton Bowl Classic, with A&M playing defending National Champion Centre College in the first postseason game in the southwest.

An underdog Aggie team was defeating a team that had allowed fewer than six points per game. But one by one, Aggie players had to be pulled from the game. By halftime Coach D.X. Bible feared he wouldn't have enough men to finish the game, so he sent someone into the stands to find E. King Gill, a student who had left football after the regular season to play basketball and who, at the moment, was spotting players for a Waco newspaper.

With no player dressing rooms in the stadium, Gill went under the stands and donned the uniform of injured player Heine Weir. Although he did not actually play in the game, his readiness to play symbolized the willingness of all Aggies to support their team to the point of actually entering the game. When the game ended in a 22–14 Aggie victory, Gill was the only Aggie left standing on the sidelines. Gill later said, "I wish I could say that I went in and ran for the winning touchdown, but I did not. I simply stood by in case my team needed me."

Since that game Aggie football fans have called themselves the 12th Man, meaning they are there to support the 11 players on the field. To further symbolize their "readiness, desire, and enthusiasm," the entire student body stands throughout the game.

In the 1980s, the tradition was expanded as coach Jackie Sherrill created the 12th Man squad. Composed solely of walk-on players, the squad would take the field for special teams' performances. This squad never allowed a kickoff return for a touchdown. Sherrill's successor, R.C. Slocum, amended the tradition in the 1990s to allow one walk-on player, wearing the No. 12 jersey, to take the field for special teams' plays.

QUESTION 1: What is the official seating capacity of Kyle Field?
   a) 85,500
   b) 83,002
   c) 82,100
   d) 85,000

QUESTION 2: What former Aggie standout was voted into the NFL Hall of Fame in 1979?
   a) John David Crow
   b) Joel Hunt
   c) Yale Lary
   d) Bob Goode

QUESTION 3: What was the name of the original 12th Man who was called from the stands to play because of a shortage of

players?
a) King Gill
b) Pinky Downs
c) Barney Welch
d) Charley Moran

QUESTION 4: In what year was the Big 12 formed?
a) 1996
b) 1992
c) 2001
d) 1998

QUESTION 5: The Aggies played two games in their first season in 1894. One was against Texas. Who was the other team?
a) Austin College
b) Houston High School
c) Fort Worth University
d) Ball High School

QUESTION 6: What Aggie receiver's father was a standout safety for A&M and later for the San Francisco 49'ers?
a) Robert Ferguson
b) Jeff Fuller
c) Chris Cole
d) Martellus Bennett

QUESTION 7: In 2005 an Aggie receiver became the first player since 1969 to letter in both football and basketball. Who was that player?
a) Jason Carter
b) Martellus Bennett
c) Kerry Franks
d) Bethel Johnson

QUESTION 8: Which former All-American for the Aggies is the only player to come out of a Texas six-man football high

school?
a) Dat Nyguen
b) Ed Simonini
c) Jack Pardee
d) Johnny Holland

QUESTION 9: What player was sworn into the U.S. Army during halftime of the 1942 Cotton Bowl?
a) John Kimbrough
b) Martin Ruby
c) Bill Sibley
d) Dick Todd

QUESTION 10: Which Aggie All-American was later elected as a Texas State Legislator?
a) John Kimbrough
b) Joe Routt
c) Tuck Chapin
d) John David Crow

QUESTION 11: Edwin Jackson Kyle, Kyle Field's namesake, held what position at A&M?
a) University President
b) Professor of Horticulture
c) Football coach
d) Held no position at school

QUESTION 12: What breed of dog is the Aggie mascot?
a) German Shepherd
b) English Bulldog
c) Collie
d) Labrador

QUESTION 13: What former All-American served as the Texas A&M Athletic director?
a) Dat Nuygen
b) Dave Elmendorf

c) Ed Simonini
d) John David Crow

QUESTION 14: What is the title of the official Aggie school song?
a) "We Are The Aggies"
b) "The Spirit of Aggieland"
c) "Hullaboo Caneck Caneck"
d) "Gig 'Em Aggies"

QUESTION 15: Which former All-American running back starred in the Hollywood movie "Lone Star Ranger"?
a) Bob Goode
b) Dick Todd
c) John David Crow
d) John Kimbrough

QUESTION 16: Which All-American lineman was killed during the WWII Battle of the Bulge?
a) Martin Ruby
b) Joe Boring
c) Bill Sibley
d) Joe Routt

QUESTION 17: Who was the first African American to be in the Aggie starting lineup?
a) Sam Williams
b) Hugh McElroy
c) J.T. Reynolds
d) Curtis Dickey

QUESTION 18: What team was the Aggie opponent when the Kyle Field attendance record was set?
a) Texas
b) Texas Tech
c) Nebraska
d) Oklahoma

QUESTION 19: What Texas A&M grad became the most recognizable referee in the NFL because of his distinctive, drawn out Texas drawl of "First Down"?
a) Ed Hochuli
b) Bill Carollo
c) Pat Haggerty
d) Mason (Red) Cashion

QUESTION 20: What school rivalry has become known as the Lone Star Showdown?
a) Texas Tech
b) Texas
c) Baylor
d) TCU

QUESTION 21: What is the name of the Aggie mascot?
a) Old Army
b) Reveille
c) Top Dog
d) King

QUESTION 22: What former lineman played for the Randolph Field Ramblers in the 1944 Cotton Bowl against the University of Texas?
a) Joe Routt
b) Marshall Robnett
c) Martin Ruby
d) Jack Little

QUESTION 23: Construction began on the original Kyle Field in:
a) 1922
b) 1927
c) 1932
d) 1935

QUESTION 24: What is the annual game against Baylor called?

a) The Lone Star Toss-Up
b) Battle of the Brazos
c) Texas Shootout
d) The Texas Cup

QUESTION 25: In the 12th Man Tradition the student body does what during the game?
a) Stand the entire game
b) Try to disrupt the opponents play calling
c) Wave white towels
d) Tear down the goal post

QUESTION 26: In what year was the tragic collapse of the traditional Aggie Bonfire?
a) 1997
b) 1998
c) 1999
d) 2000

QUESTION 27: The annual bonfire is held before which game?
a) Texas Tech
b) Oklahoma
c) Nebraska
d) Texas

QUESTION 28: What player was the 1st round draft choice of the Atlanta Falcons in 1976?
a) Bubba Bean
b) Pat Thomas
c) Garth Ten Napel
d) Curtis Dickey

QUESTION 29: What Aggie end was also a silver medal winner in the 1952 Summer Olympics?
a) Ollie Matson
b) Randy Matson

    c) Darrow Hooper
    d) Walt Davis

QUESTION 30: What is the name of the cannon that's fired after every Aggie touchdown?
    a) Big Betsy
    b) Big Bertha
    c) The Spirit of '02
    d) Old Army

QUESTION 31: What year was the first on-campus bonfire?
    a) 1920
    b) 1935
    c) 1909
    d) 1895

Chapter 2

The Team

OVER THE YEARS Texas A&M has fielded many good teams, but arguably the best was the 1939 National Champions. This is saying a lot when you consider that during the long ago 1917 and 1919 seasons the Aggies didn't allow a single point to be scored against them, outscoring their opponents 270-0 in 1917 and 275-0 in 1919. These were the days of leather helmets and minimal protective pads and these were some tough guys but they didn't play the game in the way we know it now.

The 1939 team, coached by a former baseball coach by the name of Homer Norton was different. Led by their All-American running back, "Jarring" John Kimbrough they defeated some of footballs best teams, including TCU, who had been the 1938 National Champions. Led by All-American lineman Marshall Robnett, the Aggies led the nation in scoring and rushing defense and set an NCAA record for fewest yards allowed per game ... an astounding 76.3 yards. By the end of the regular season the Aggies had outscored their opponents 212-18 and in the Sugar Bowl game, solidified their hold as #1 in the nation by defeating a very good Tulane team 14-13.

In more recent times, Aggie teams coached by Jackie Sherrill in 1985, '86, '87 and R.C. Slocum in '91, '92, and '93 were other outstanding teams. In the 1985, '86, and '87 seasons the Aggies lost only three conference games and played in three successive Cotton Bowls, beating a Bo Jackson led Auburn in 1985. During the 1991, '92, and '93 seasons, the Aggies also went to three consecutive Cotton Bowls and were undefeated in conference play.

In the 2011 season, the Aggies closed out their season with six straight wins and a three-way tie for the Big 12 South title.

QUESTION 32: What is the Aggie overtime record at Kyle Field?
a) 5-2
b) 7-1
c) 8-0
d) 5-0

QUESTION 33: The Aggies have played the most non-conference games against which opponent?
a) Alabama
b) UCLA
c) LSU
d) Clemson

QUESTION 34: How many years were the Aggies a member of the Southwest Conference?
a) 75
b) 62
c) 80
d) 54

QUESTION 35: Which team ended the Aggies longest regular season unbeaten streak of 23 games in 1993?
a) Oklahoma
b) Texas
c) Rice
d) Arkansas

QUESTION 36: When was the last time a blocked punt by the Aggies was returned for a touchdown?
a) 2009 vs. Colorado
b) 2005 vs. SMU
c) 2007 vs. Texas Tech
d) 2010 vs. Texas

QUESTION 37: When the Aggies won the 1939 National Championship what other SWC team did they replace as the 1938 Champion?
- a) Texas
- b) TCU
- c) Arkansas
- d) Rice

QUESTION 38: The most touchdowns scored by the Aggies in a single game is 11. Who was the opponent?
- a) Clemson
- b) SMU
- c) Miami (Fla)
- d) TCU

QUESTION 39: The Aggies first played Arkansas in what year?
- a) 1903
- b) 1940
- c) 1920
- d) 1917

QUESTION 40: The Aggies have played one game with three overtimes. Who was the opponent?
- a) Texas
- b) Fresno State
- c) Baylor
- d) Penn State

QUESTION 41: What is the longest win streak for the Aggies while a member of the SWC?
- a) 26
- b) 20
- c) 19
- d) 14

QUESTION 42: How many times have the Aggies been ranked

first in the nation (AP Poll)?
   a) 5
   b) 10
   c) 7
   d) 9

QUESTION 43: In the 2002 season an unranked Aggie team upset the #1 team in the nation. Who was that team?
   a) Oklahoma
   b) Nebraska
   c) Texas
   d) Alabama

QUESTION 44: Who were the twin brothers on the 2010 Aggie roster?
   a) Eddie Brown/Kenny Brown
   b) Luke Jocekel/Matt Jocekel
   c) Jerrod Johnson/Malcolm Johnson
   d) Brandon Jackson/Brandel Jackson

QUESTION 45: When was the last time the Aggies had an unbeaten, untied season?
   a) 1998
   b) 1991
   c) 1956
   d) 1939

QUESTION 46: In 1920 the Aggies scored 110 points in a single game. Who was the opponent?
   a) Sam Houston St
   b) Austin College
   c) Daniel Baker
   d) Sewanee

QUESTION 47: In which season did the Aggies have their highest home game average attendance of 87,711 per game?

a) 2009
b) 2010
c) 2001
d) 2002

QUESTION 48: The highest attendance of any 2010 game (home or away) was the game against which team?
a) Texas Tech
b) Oklahoma
c) Oklahoma St
d) Texas

QUESTION 49: Which team was the opponent when the 12th Man tradition was born?
a) Texas
b) Centre College
c) Fordham
d) Baylor

QUESTION 50: During the 2010 season the Aggies had a single game high of 623 yards of total offense against which team?
a) Texas Tech
b) Louisiana Tech
c) Baylor
d) Oklahoma St.

QUESTION 51: What was the Aggie conference won-loss record in 2010?
a) 5-4
b) 6-3
c) 7-2
d) 8-2

QUESTION 52: The Aggies longest regular season win streak is?
    a) 19
    b) 23
    c) 17
    d) 25

QUESTION 53: In what year did the Aggies play their archrival Texas for the first time?
    a) 1920
    b) 1901
    c) 1894
    d) 1876

QUESTION 54: What was the Aggies overall won-loss record in 2010?
    a) 9-4
    b) 10-2
    c) 8-4
    d) 7-6

QUESTION 55: During the 1986 season the Aggies had a record 38 first downs in a single game. Who was the opponent?
    a) Texas Tech
    b) Texas
    c) TCU
    d) SMU

QUESTION 56: How many times did the Aggies win the Southwest Conference title (1915-1995)?
    a) 21
    b) 17
    c) 27
    d) 32

QUESTION 57: What is the longest punt return in team history?
    a) 100 yards
    b) 98 yards

c) 87 yards.
d) 95 yards.

QUESTION 58: Which team is a first-time opponent scheduled for the 2011 season?
a) Nevada
b) Idaho
c) Montana St.
d) McNeese St.

Chapter 3

The Players

OVER THE YEARS many great players have worn the Aggie maroon and white, winning many accolades and numerous awards. In the early years, John Kimbrough, Marshall Robnett, Joel Hunt, Joe Routt and Martin Ruby were All-American players. Yale Lary, a baseball and football star at A&M who is considered one of the all-time best defensive backs and punters, was elected to the NFL Hall of Fame in 1979. Running back John David Crow was a Heisman Trophy winner and 42 other Aggies have received All-American honors.

Jack Pardee, a product of Bear Bryant's Junction Boy's training camp, is the only player to come out of a six-man high school football program and go on to be a player or coach in the NFL, World Football League, United States Football League, and the Canadian Football League. Tony Franklin is the only college player to kick two field goals of over 60 yards in one game, and holds 18 NCAA records for kicking.

In more recent years the Aggies have produced many players that are well known to NFL fans. Defensive tackle Ray Childress was a perennial All-Pro. Among others, Charlie Kruger, Lester Hayes, Jacob Green, Seth McKinney, Sam Adams, Dat Nyguen and Aaron Glenn excelled at A&M and as NFL players after their collegiate careers ended.

The 2010 season continued the tradition of producing outstanding players with linebacker Von Miller being picked as the #2 overall selection in the NFL draft and the stellar play of wide receiver Jeff Fuller and running back Cyrus Grey, both of whom return in 2011. In all, the Aggies have 18 starters on offense and defense returning in 2011, and, after ending the season with a six-game conference winning streak, are poised to make a run at a Big 12 Championship.

QUESTION 59: In his first start as the Aggie QB during the 2010 season, Ryan Tannehill passed for 449 yards. Which team was the opponent?
  a) Texas Tech
  b) Kansas St.
  c) Missouri
  d) Colorado

QUESTION 60: What player is the career leader in punt return yards?
  a) Marion Flanagan
  b) Dick Todd
  c) Dante Hall
  d) Rod Harris

QUESTION 61: What player holds the team record for most punt return yards in a single season?
  a) Marion Flanagan
  b) Dick Todd
  c) Dante Hall
  d) Rod Harris

QUESTION 62: When Jerrod Johnson set a new team career pass completion record, who's record did he break?
  a) Stephen McGee
  b) Cory Pullig
  c) Kevin Murray
  d) Reggie McNeal

QUESTION 63: During the 2010 season the most tackles in a single game (19) were made by?
  a) Von Miller
  b) Michael Hodges

c) Damontre Moore
d) Trent Hunter

QUESTION 64: Which player had the longest rushing TD in the 2010 season?
a) Ryan Swope
b) Christine Michael
c) Jerrod Johnson
d) Cyrus Gray

QUESTION 65: What player is the Aggie career scoring leader?
a) Darren Lewis
b) Joel Hunt
c) Tony Franklin
d) Kyle Bryant

QUESTION 66: Which Aggie QB had the most passes intercepted during his career?
a) Jerrod Johnson
b) Gary Kubiak
c) Ed Hargett
d) Reggie McNeal

QUESTION 67: How many consecutive 100 yard rushing games did Cyrus Gray have in 2010?
a) 4
b) 5
c) 6
d) 7

QUESTION 68: Which Aggie QB holds the team record for most 100 yard rushing games?
a) Reggie McNeal
b) Stephen McGee
c) Jerrod Johnson
d) Babe Hallmark

QUESTION 69: Who is the only Aggie freshman to rush for over 200 yards in a single game?
- a) Dante Hall
- b) Darren Lewis
- c) Leeland McElroy
- d) Greg Hill

QUESTION 70: Which player holds the team record in career rushing touchdowns?
- a) Jevorski Lane
- b) Leeland McElroy
- c) Curtis Dickey
- d) Darren Lewis

QUESTION 71: In the 2010 season the longest run for a touchdown was made by?
- a) Christine Michael
- b) Cyrus Gray
- c) Ryan Tannehill
- d) Jerrod Johnson

QUESTION 72: Which player holds the team career record for average yards per punt?
- a) Shane Lechler
- b) Justin Brantly
- c) Bob Goode
- d) Yale Lary

QUESTION 73: Which Aggie QB holds the team record for most career TD passes?
- a) Ryan Tannehill
- b) Jerrod Johnson
- c) Stephen McGee
- d) Kevin Murray

QUESTION 74: Which receiver holds the team record for career touchdown receptions?

a) Bob Long
b) Albert Connell
c) Bethel Johnson
d) Jeff Fuller

QUESTION 75: The leader in all-purpose yards for the 2010 season was?
a) Christine Michael
b) Jerrod Johnson
c) Cyrus Gray
d) Ryan Tannehill

QUESTION 76: Through the 2010 season who is the all-time leader in receiving yards?
a) Robert Ferguson
b) Albert Connell
c) Terrence Murphy
d) Jeff Fuller

QUESTION 77: What former standout running back was the NCAA 60 yard dash champion for three consecutive years in 1978, 1979, and 1980?
a) Curtis Dickey
b) Bubba Bean
c) Greg Hill
d) Johnny Hector

QUESTION 78: Who is the career interception leader?
a) Kevin Smith
b) Dave Elmendorf
c) Aaron Glenn
d) Lester Hayes

QUESTION 79: Which player had a 100 yard kickoff return for a TD in 2010?
a) Cyrus Gray
b) Ryan Swope

c) Coryell Judie
d) Christine Michael

QUESTION 80: What player is the career leader in total offense?
a) Reggie McNeal
b) John Kimbrough
c) Jerrod Johnson
d) Bob Smith

QUESTION 81: What player is the career leader in pass completion percentage?
a) Stephen McGee
b) Reggie McNeal
c) Jerrod Johnson
d) Billy Tidwell

QUESTION 82: Which QB has the most TD passes in a season?
a) Jerrod Johnson
b) Dick Gardemal
c) Stephen McGee
d) Kevin Murray

QUESTION 83: Which Aggie defensive back was a 1st round draft choice of Dallas Cowboys in 1992?
a) Patrick Bates
b) Kevin Smith
c) Lester Hayes
d) Aaron Glenn

QUESTION 84: Which player was named team MVP in 1997?
a) Dat Nyguen
b) Robert Ferguson
c) Dante Hall
d) Ja'mar Toombs

QUESTION 85: Which player is the single season leader in all-purpose yards (rushing, receiving, kick returns, punt returns)?

a) Darren Lewis
b) Cyrus Gray
c) Leeland McElroy
d) Greg Hill

QUESTION 86: Which kicker has the team record longest field goal of 65 yards?
a) Todd Pegram
b) Tony Franklin
c) Randy Bullock
d) Terrence Kitchens

QUESTION 87: What player holds the team single game rushing record?
a) Christine Michael
b) Curtis Dickey
c) Bob Smith
d) Darren Lewis

QUESTION 88: The longest punt in Aggie history is 86 yards. Who was the punter?
a) Shane Lechler
b) Bobby Goff
c) Justin Brantley
d) Cody Scales

QUESTION 89: Who is the Aggie all-time scoring leader?
a) Darren Lewis
b) Joel Hunt
c) Tony Franklin
d) Kyle Bryant

QUESTION 90: What Aggie is the career leader in kick-off return yards?
a) Kerry Franks
b) Dave Elmendorf

c) Terrence Murphy
d) Cyrus Gray

QUESTION 91: Which player is the all-time statistical leader in average yards per punt return?
a) Cyrus Gray
b) Aaron Glenn
c) Bethel Johnson
d) Jordon Pugh

QUESTION 92: Which player has the most interceptions (4) in a single game?
a) Lester Hayes
b) Pat Thomas
c) Joe Boring
d) Kevin Smith

QUESTION 93: Which running back holds the season record for best average yards gained per carry?
a) Curtis Dickey
b) Darren Lewis
c) Dante Hall
d) Courtney Lewis

QUESTION 94: Who is the Aggie career leader in tackles?
a) Dat Nyguen
b) Johnny Holland
c) Ed Simonini
d) Ray Childress

QUESTION 95: The season record for rushing attempts is held by?
a) Greg Hill
b) George Woodward
c) Roger Vick
d) Darren Lewis

QUESTION 96: Von Miller had 17 QB sacks in 2010. Who's record did he tie?
a) Jacob Green
b) Jack Pardee
c) Monte Moncrief
d) Jim Flowers

QUESTION 97: The most punts in a single game is 17. Who was the punter?
a) Shane Lechler
b) Justin Brantly
c) Bob Goode
d) David Appleby

QUESTION 98: The team record for most extra points in a single game is?
a) 7
b) 9
c) 6
d) 10

QUESTION 99: Who was the kicker in question 98?
a) Larry Talbot
b) Terry Venetoulies
c) Kyle Bryant
d) Todd Pegram

QUESTION 100: Which receiver led the team in number of receptions in a single game of the 2010 season?
a) Ryan Swope
b) Jeff Fuller
c) Uzoma Nwachukwu
d) Michael Lamonte

QUESTION 101: The season record for most yards rushing by a

freshman is held by?
   a) Greg Hill
   b) Mike Goodson
   c) Crus Gray
   d) Glen Lippman

QUESTION 102: During the 2010 season the longest run from scrimmage for a touchdown was 84 yards. Who was the player?
   a) Christine Michael
   b) Cyrus Gray
   c) Ryan Tannehill
   d) Jerrod Johnson

QUESTION 103: Which Aggie QB holds the team record for the most passing attempts in a single game?
   a) Brandon Stewart
   b) Jerrod Johnson
   c) Edd Hargett
   d) Kevin Murray

QUESTION 104: During the 2010 season the longest reception for a touchdown was made by which player?
   a) Jeff Fuller
   b) Uzoma Nwachekwu
   c) Ryan Swope
   d) Kenric McNeal

QUESTION 105: Which player holds the freshman record for kickoff return total yards?
   a) Terrence Murphy
   b) Kerry Franks
   c) Sirr Parker
   d) Cyrus Gray

QUESTION 106: Which player holds the single season receiving record?

a) Albert Connell
b) Jeff Fuller
c) Robert Ferguson
d) Mike Goodson

QUESTION 107: The player with the most unassisted tackles in the 2010 season was?
a) Von Miller
b) Michael Hodges
c) Judie Coryell
d) Garrick Williams

QUESTION 108: Through the 2010 season which player holds the record for most 100 yard receiving games?
a) Albert Connell
b) Ken McLean
c) Jeff Fuller
d) Terrance Murphy

QUESTION 109: Which Aggie punter led the Big 12 in punting for three consecutive years, 1997-1999?
a) Cody Scales
b) Sean Terry
c) Shane Lechler
d) David Appleby

QUESTION 110: Which kicker has the highest season percentage of field goals made?
a) Kyle Bryant
b) Todd Pegram
c) Tony Franklin
d) Scott Slater

QUESTION 111: Which player holds the team record for most rushing attempts in a single game?
a) Mark Green
b) Johhny Hector

c) Dante Hall
d) Roger Vick

QUESTION 112: Which kicker was the last to kick four field goals in a single game?
a) Tony Franklin
b) Randy Bullock
c) Todd Pegram
d) Terrence Kitchens

QUESTION 113: Who holds the freshman record for most total yards in punt returns?
a) Marion Flanagan
b) Dante Hall
c) Billy Cannon
d) Aaron Glenn

QUESTION 114: Which player has the most yards in kickoff returns in a season?
a) Carl Roaches
b) Coryell Judie
c) Kerry Franks
d) Cyrus Gray

QUESTION 115: The single game TDs scored by passing is seven. Who was the QB?
a) Jerrod Johnson
b) Stephen McGee
c) Dustin Long
d) Jeff Granger

QUESTION 116: The team record for most kickoff returns in a single game is held by?
a) Cyrus Gray
b) Leland McElroy
c) Kerry Franks
d) Bob Smith

QUESTION 117: What freshman running back holds the team record for longest run from scrimmage?
a) Courtney Lewis
b) Christine Michael
c) Rodney Thomas
d) Cyrus Gray

QUESTION 118: Cyrus Gray had a season high 223 yards rushing in a game. Which Big 12 team was the opponent?
a) Texas
b) Baylor
c) Texas Tech
d) Oklahoma St.

QUESTION 119: What Aggie running back was a 1st round draft choice of the Washington Redskins in 1949?
a) Dick Todd
b) Andy Hillhouse
c) Glenn Lippman
d) Bob Goode

QUESTION 120: Which Aggie kicker had two field goals of over 60 yards in one game?
a) Randy Bullock
b) Dusty Mangum
c) Tony Franklin
d) Terrence Kitchins

QUESTION 121: Which player holds the team and old SWC record for most punt returns in a single game?
a) Dante Hall
b) Charlie Royalty
c) Carl Roaches
d) Rod Harris

QUESTION 122: When Cyrus Gray set a new season record of all-purpose yards in 2010, who's record did he break?
a) Darren Lewis
b) Leeland McElroy
c) Dante Hall
d) Jason Carter

QUESTION 123: Who is the only QB to have over 2,000 yards rushing in his career at A&M?
a) Stephen McGee
b) Bucky Richardson
c) Jerrod Johnson
d) Reggie McNeal

QUESTION 124: Which Aggie player won the Heisman Trophy in 1957?
a) Jack Pardee
b) John David Crow
c) Charlie Krueger
d) Jack Little

QUESTION 125: What player holds the team record for most points scored in a bowl game?
a) Ja'mar Toombs
b) John Kimbrough
c) John David Crow
d) George Woodward

QUESTION 126: What player holds the career record for most yards per catch as a receiver?
a) Chris Cole
b) Marcellus Bennett
c) Albert Connell
d) Mike Whitwell

QUESTION 127: Which player holds the team record for most receptions by a freshman?

a) Jeff Fuller
b) Robert Ferguson
c) Ryan Tannehill
d) Rod Bernstein

QUESTION 128: Which player holds the team record for most receptions by a sophomore?
a) Robert Ferguson
b) Ryan Tannehill
c) Albert Connell
d) Jamaar Taylor

QUESTION 129: Which QB has the most touchdown passes in a single game?
a) Dustin Long
b) Gary Kubiak
c) Reggie McNeal
d) Jerrod Johnson

Chapter 4

The Coaches

THERE'S NO DOUBT that the coach is the heart and soul of any team. A good coach is able to recruit the best players. A good coach can take a good player and make him a great player. A good coach molds a player's character as well as his playing skills. And a coach wins games when he probably shouldn't.

The Aggies have had 28 different head coaches, with one of those 28 serving two different tenures. For present day fans, the most notable is R.C. Slocum who was head coach for 14 seasons and compiled an outstanding 123-47-2 record and is one of the few head coaches in NCAA history to never have a losing season.

During the SWC era, head coach Homer Norton also led the Aggies for 14 seasons and was the coach during the Aggies National Championship season in 1939. Other notable coaches to lead the Aggies were D.X. Bible, Matty Bell, Gene Stallings, Emory Ballard and Paul (Bear) Bryant.

Of those, the best known was Bear Bryant, who coached the Aggies from 1954-1957 before returning to his alma mater the University of Alabama.

When Bryant took over as head coach prior to the 1954 season, he decided the Aggie players were weak and not trained properly and decided to run a "boot camp" in the hot, dusty, west Texas town of Junction. The infamous ten-day training camp at Junction, Texas in September 1954 has been memorialized in the book and movie *The Junction Boys*. On a field scratched out of the hard dirt, mostly devoid of grass, he conducted daily drills from before dawn until well after dark. Of the approximate 100 players who reported to camp, 37 "survived." Among those, two players, Jack Pardee and Gene Stallings, went on to have successful careers as head coaches themselves.

During his coaching career, Bryant won six national and 13 conference titles. When he retired, Bryant had the most wins as a head coach in collegiate history.

Who is the best coach in Aggie history?

It all depends on your viewpoint: R.C. Slocum's winning percentage or Homer Norton's National Championship. Take your pick, but it's hard to overlook D.X. Bible's unbeaten, unscored upon season.

QUESTION 130: The term "wrecking crew" was the name given the Aggie defense during the tenure of which head coach?
a) Homer Norton
b) Gene Stallings
c) R.C. Slocum
d) Dennis Franchione

QUESTION 131: How many years did R.C. Slocum serve as the head coach?
a) 10
b) 15
c) 14
d) 12

QUESTION 132: What current Aggie assistant coach played in Super Bowl XXXVII for the Oakland Raiders in 2003?
a) Nick Toth
b) Tim DeRuyter
c) Randy Jordan
d) Charles McMillian

QUESTION 133: Which head coach was also the Aggie basketball head coach?
a) Matty Bell
b) Homer Norton
c) C.B. Moran
d) D.X. Bible

QUESTION 134: Which former Aggie player was an assistant coach for the Dallas Cowboys?
a) Jack Pardee
b) Gene Stallings
c) Dat Nyguen
d) Dave Elmendorf

QUESTION 135: In which year and under which head coach were the Aggies National Champions?
a) Paul (Bear) Bryant – 1956
b) D.X. Bible – 1924
c) Homer Norton – 1939
d) Matty Bell – 1933

QUESTION 136: How many bowl games did the Aggies play under coach R.C. Slocum?
a) 10
b) 11
c) 13
d) 15

QUESTION 137: Where did coach Mike Sherman play college football?
a) Alcorn St.
b) Ohio St.
c) Central Connecticut
d) Purdue

QUESTION 138: Which Aggie coach originated the 12th Man kickoff team?
a) Bear Bryant
b) R.C. Slocum
c) Emory Ballard
d) Jackie Sherrill

QUESTION 139: Which Aggie coach is generally recognized for

designing the wishbone offense?
a) Emory Ballard
b) R.C. Slocum
c) Jackie Sherrill
d) Dennis Franchione

QUESTION 140: Who was the head coach during the infamous "Junction Boys" training camp?
a) Gene Stallings
b) Bear Bryant
c) Emory Ballard
d) Dennis Franchione

QUESTION 141: Who was the 1977 defensive end that became head coach of SMU?
a) Aaron Glenn
b) Jason Webster
c) Phil Bennett
d) Jack Pardee

QUESTION 142: Coach Mike Sherman was a coach (head or assistant) for which NFL team?
a) Houston Texans
b) Green Bay Packers
c) Seattle Seahawks
d) All of the above

QUESTION 143: Who has the most career wins as the A&M head coach?
a) Jackie Sherrill
b) Bear Bryant
c) D.V. Graves
d) R.C. Slocum

QUESTION 144: How many times was R.C. Slocum named SWC Coach of the Year?

a) 5
b) 8
c) 3
d) 4

QUESTION 145: How many head coaches have the Aggies had?
a) 29
b) 19
c) 22
d) 15

QUESTION 146: Who was the head coach during their unbeaten, untied 1939 season?
a) Homer Norton
b) D.X. Bible
c) Matty Bell
d) Harry Stiteler

QUESTION 147: What former player was the head coach for the Houston Texans?
a) Willie Zaplac
b) Jim Flowers
c) Joel Hunt
d) Gary Kubiak

QUESTION 148: Which 2010 assistant coach played defensive back for the Air Force Academy?
a) Charles McMillian
b) Tim DeRuyter
c) Nick Toth
d) Tom Rossley

QUESTION 149: In the 1919 season the Aggies outscored their opponents 275-0. Who was the head coach?
a) Homer Norton
b) Matty Bell

c) D.X. Bible
d) D.V. Graves

QUESTION 150: Which former coach was elected to the College Football Hall of Fame in 1951?
a) Homer Norton
b) D.X. Bible
c) Matty Bell
d) Emory Ballard

QUESTION 151: What was D.X. Bible's middle name?
a) Xavier
b) Xenophon
c) Xerxes
d) No middle name – just an initial

QUESTION 152: Which Aggie head coach was a two-time All-American at the United States Military Academy (West Point)?
a) Raymond George
b) Jim Myers
c) Tom Wilson
d) Hank Foldberg

QUESTION 153: Who was the head coach in the 1983 Cotton Bowl when A&M defeated an Auburn team led by Heisman Trophy winner Bo Jackson?
a) Emory Ballard
b) Tom Wilson
c) Jackie Sherrill
d) R.C. Slocum

QUESTION 154: What former coach was a "survivor" of the 1954 "Junction Boys" training camp?
a) Gene Stallings
b) Jack Pardee

c) R.C. Slocum
d) Emory Ballard

QUESTION 155: Where did coach Bear Bryant play college football?
a) Mississippi St.
b) LSU
c) Auburn
d) Alabama

QUESTION 156: Where did Coach R.C. Slocum play college football?
a) LSU
b) Southwest Louisiana
c) McNeese State
d) Hardin Simmons

QUESTION 157: Of the 111 players who reported to the infamous "Junction Boys" training camp, how many quit within ten days?
a) 25
b) 52
c) 76
d) 44

QUESTION 158: The Aggies won the SWC for three consecutive years, 1985-1987. Who was the head coach during those years?
a) Jackie Sherrill
b) R.C. Slocum
c) Gene Stallings
d) Tom Wilson

QUESTION 159: Who did Jim Myers replace as head coach?
a) Harry Stiteler
b) Gene Stallings

c) Raymond George
d) Bear Bryant

QUESTION 160: What Aggie head coach played minor league baseball for the Birmingham Barons before becoming a football coach?
a) Matty Bell
b) Homer Norton
c) Tom Wilson
d) Jackie Sherrill

Chapter 5

The Bowls and other Superlatives

THE FIRST BOWL game Texas A&M played in was the 1922 Dixie Classic against then football powerhouse Centre College. Altogether, the Aggies have played in a total 32 bowl games, including 17 as SWC Champions in the Cotton Bowl. Other major bowl appearances include the Sugar Bowl, Sun Bowl, Orange Bowl, Alamo Bowl, Holiday Bowl, Independence Bowl and Liberty Bowl.

The most important bowl game the Aggies have ever played was the 1940 Sugar Bowl, when #1 ranked A&M defeated #6 ranked Tulane 14-13 on the strength of John Kimbrough's running and a blocked extra point by the smallest player on the Aggie team, 5' 8" Herbie Smith.

The most memorable was the 1968 Cotton Bowl when teacher faced student. Aggie head coach Gene Stallings led his team to a 20-16 victory over Alabama, coached by his former coach and mentor, Bear Bryant. After the game Bryant carried Stallings off the field on his shoulders. The dullest was perhaps the 1942 Cotton Bowl when A&M defeated Alabama 3-0 and both teams only had three first downs between them.

Currently, three Aggie players hold NCAA bowl records. In the 1990 Holiday Bowl, Layne Talbot attempted and made nine extra points. In the 1950 Presidential Cup, Bob Smith set the record for highest kickoff return average of 60.5 yards per return (two) and in the 2007 Alamo Bowl Justin Brantly averaged 55 yards per punt (six).

QUESTION 161: While members of the SWC the Aggies played the same team three times in the Cotton Bowl Classic. Who was that team?
   a) LSU
   b) Notre Dame

  c) Alabama
  d) Mississippi St.

QUESTION 162: Which Aggie player holds the NCAA record for highest kickoff return average in a bowl game?
  a) Bob Smith
  b) Bob Goode
  c) Cyrus Gray
  d) Yale Lary

QUESTION 163: What team was the Aggies opponent in their first bowl game?
  a) SMU
  b) Texas
  c) Centre
  d) Clemson

QUESTION 164: Through the 2010 season, how many times have the Aggies played in the Cotton Bowl Classic?
  a) 12
  b) 9
  c) 16
  d) 20

QUESTION 165: Who was the Aggie opponent in the 1939 Sugar Bowl?
  a) Alabama
  b) Georgia
  c) Tulane
  d) Florida State

QUESTION 166: What player holds the team record for most points scored in a bowl game?
  a) Ja'Mar Toombs
  b) John Kimbrough
  c) John David Crow
  d) George Woodward

QUESTION 167: Which team was the Aggie opponent in the 1940 Cotton Bowl Classic?
a) LSU
b) Tulane
c) USC
d) Fordham

QUESTION 168: Which Aggie QB is the career bowl leader (all bowls played in) in yards passing?
a) Kevin Murray
b) Jerrod Johnson
c) Cory Pullig
d) Stephen McGee

QUESTION 169: The Aggies hold the NCAA record for fewest first downs allowed in a bowl game. In what game and against what opponent was that record set?
a) 1988 Cotton Bowl vs. Notre Dame
b) 1992 Cotton Bowl vs. Florida State
c) 1977 Bluebonnet Bowl vs. USC
d) 1941 Cotton Bowl vs. Alabama

QUESTION 170: Which former player and coach was a 2010 inductee into the College Football Hall of Fame?
a) Jack Pardee
b) Gene Stallings
c) Hank Foldberg
d) Jim Myers

QUESTION 171: In the 2001 Gallery Furniture Bowl the Aggies held their opponent to -26 yards rushing. Who was that team?
a) Iowa State
b) Notre Dame
c) TCU
d) BYU

QUESTION 172: Which Aggie QB has the most passing yards in a bowl game?
a) Jerrod Johnson
b) Kevin Murray
c) Gary Kubiak
d) Reggie McNeal

QUESTION 173: Who is the only Aggie player named to the first team All-Big 12 three times?
a) Seth McKinney
b) Terrence Murphy
c) Shane Lechler
d) Dat Nyguen

QUESTION174: Who was the first Aggie player to be named All-American?
a) Hank Flodberg
b) Joe Routt
c) John Kimbrough
d) Joel Hunt

QUESTION 175: Which Aggie player received the Lombardi Award in 1998?
a) Dat Nyguen
b) Sam Adams
c) Johhny Holland
d) Brian Gamble

QUESTION 176: Which former Aggie was named All-Pro six times as a Houston Oiler?
a) John Roper
b) Marcus Buckley
c) Alex Morris
d) Ray Childress

QUESTION 177: The first bowl game played by the Aggies was?

a) Sugar Bowl
b) Dixie Classic
c) Texas Bowl
d) Gator Bowl

QUESTION 178: Which player holds the team record for most rushing yards in a bowl game?
a) Ja'Mar Toombs
b) Curtis Dickey
c) George Woodward
d) Bucky Richardson

QUESTION 179: What is the total number of bowl games that the Aggies have played in?
a) 32
b) 29
c) 18
d) 40

QUESTION 180: What former Aggie was the starting linebacker for the Green Bay Packers in Super Bowl I?
a) Sam Adams
b) Lee Roy Caffey
c) Domingo Bryant
d) Mike Little

QUESTION 181: Which Aggie player won the 2010 Butkus Award?
a) Tony Jerod-Eddie
b) Luke Joeckel
c) Cedrick Ogbuchi
d) Von Miller

QUESTION 182: Which former Aggie lineman was elected to the College Football Hall of Fame in 2010?
a) Sam Adams
b) Charlie Kruger

c) Ray Childress
d) Jacob Green

QUESTION 183: Which player was voted game MVP in the 1988 Cotton Bowl?
a) Kevin Murray
b) Roger Vick
c) Bucky Richardson
d) Darren Lewis

QUESTION 184: Which Aggie place kicker holds the NCAA record for most extra points made in a bowl game?
a) Tony Franklin
b) Layne Talbot
c) Scott Slater
d) Terry Venetoulius

QUESTION 185: In which bowl game did the Aggies use a "hidden player" trick play to break a scoreless tie?
a) 1941 Cotton Bowl
b) 1968 Cotton Bowl
c) 1977 Bluebonnet Bowl
d) 1987 Cotton Bowl

QUESTION 186: Which Aggie player was named the 2000 Big 12 Offensive Newcomer of the year?
a) Dat Nyguen
b) Seth McKinney
c) Jason Glenn
d) Robert Ferguson

QUESTION 187: Which player was named 2009 Big 12 Offensive Freshman of the year?
a) Cyrus Gray
b) Christine Michael
c) Jerrod Johnson
d) Jeff Fuller

QUESTION 188: In the 1990 Holiday Bowl the Aggies had 680 total yards. Who was the opponent?
a) USC
b) Auburn
c) Georgia
d) BYU

QUESTION 189: Which Aggie player is the NCAA record holder for most kickoff return yards in a bowl game?
a) Bob Goode
b) Bob Smith
c) Barney Welch
d) Dustin Harris

QUESTION 190: Which player was named to the 1st Team Big-12 Offense in 2010?
a) Randy Bullock
b) Cyrus Gray
c) Jeff Fuller
d) Michael Hodges

QUESTION 191: In the 1977 Bluebonnet Bowl the Aggies had 486 yards rushing. Who was the opponent?
a) USC
b) BYU
c) Tennessee
d) Pittsburg

QUESTION 192: Who is the only player in Texas A&M history to rush for over 5,000 yards?
a) Curtis Dickey
b) Darren Lewis
c) Dante Hall
d) George Woodward

QUESTION 193: In 1998, the Aggies played in the Kickoff Classic at Giants Stadium, in East Rutherford, NJ. What team was their opponent?
   a) Penn State
   b) Michigan State
   c) Ohio State
   d) Florida State

QUESTION 194: The most points scored by an Aggie kicker in a bowl game is 16 in the 1995 Alamo Bowl. Who was the kicker?
   a) Kyle Bryant
   b) Tony Franklin
   c) Billy Tidwell
   d) Layne Talbot

QUESTION 195: Which Aggie place kicker holds the NCAA record for longest field goal in a bowl game?
   a) Layne Talbot
   b) Tony Franklin
   c) Todd Pegram
   d) Scott Slater

QUESTION 196: Which Aggie QB was the leading rusher in both the 1988 Cotton Bowl and the 1990 Holiday Bowl?
   a) Kevin Murray
   b) Billy Tidwell
   c) Gary Kubiak
   d) Bucky Richardson

QUESTION 197: Who was the Aggies leading receiver in the 2007 Alamo Bowl?
   a) Mickey Jones
   b) Chris Taylor
   c) Martellus Bennett
   d) DeQawn Mobley

QUESTION 198: The opening kickoff of the 1950 Presidential Cup was returned 100 yards for a TD by which Aggie player?
a) Glenn Lipman
b) Bob Smith
c) Bob Goode
d) Yale Lary

QUESTION 199: The Aggies have played in one bowl game that went to overtime. Which bowl was that and who was the Aggie opponent?
a) 2000 Independence Bowl – Mississippi St.
b) 1999 Sugar Bowl – Ohio St.
c) 1989 John Hancock Bowl – Pitt
d) 1998 Cotton Bowl – UCLA

QUESTION 200: Through the 2010 season, how many times have the Aggies been a ranked team?
a) 295
b) 175
c) 306
d) 251

Texas A&M Aggies IQ Answer Key

___ **QUESTION 1:** B

___ **QUESTION 2:** C

___ **QUESTION 3:** A

___ **QUESTION 4:** A

___ **QUESTION 5:** D

___ **QUESTION 6:** B

___ **QUESTION 7:** B

___ **QUESTION 8:** C

___ **QUESTION 9:** B

___ **QUESTION 10:** A

___ **QUESTION 11:** B

___ **QUESTION 12:** C

___ **QUESTION 13:** D

___ **QUESTION 14:** B

___ **QUESTION 15:** D

___ **QUESTION 16:** D

___ **QUESTION 17:** B

___ **QUESTION 18:** C

___ **QUESTION 19:** D

___ **QUESTION 20:** B

___ **QUESTION 21:** B

___ **QUESTION 22:** C

___ **QUESTION 23:** B

___ **QUESTION 24:** B

___ **QUESTION 25:** A

___ **QUESTION 26:** C

___ **QUESTION 27:** D

___ **QUESTION 28:** A

___ **QUESTION 29:** C

___ **QUESTION 30:** C

___ **QUESTION 31:** C

___ **QUESTION 32:** A

___ **QUESTION 33:** C

___ **QUESTION 34:** C

___ **QUESTION 35:** A

___ QUESTION 36: B

___ QUESTION 37: B

___ QUESTION 38: C

___ QUESTION 39: A

___ QUESTION 40: B

___ QUESTION 41: B

___ QUESTION 42: C

___ QUESTION 43: A

___ QUESTION 44: D

___ QUESTION 45: D

___ QUESTION 46: C

___ QUESTION 47: C

___ QUESTION 48: D

___ QUESTION 49: B

___ QUESTION 50: A

___ QUESTION 51: B

___ QUESTION 52: B

___ QUESTION 53: C

___ QUESTION 54: A

___ **QUESTION 55:** D

___ **QUESTION 56:** B

___ **QUESTION 57:** B

___ **QUESTION 58:** B

___ **QUESTION 59:** A

___ **QUESTION 60:** B

___ **QUESTION 61:** C

___ **QUESTION 62:** B

___ **QUESTION 63:** B

___ **QUESTION 64:** D

___ **QUESTION 65:** D

___ **QUESTION 66:** C

___ **QUESTION 67:** C

___ **QUESTION 68:** B

___ **QUESTION 69:** D

___ **QUESTION 70:** A

___ **QUESTION 71:** B

___ **QUESTION 72:** A

___ **QUESTION 73:** B

___ **QUESTION 74:** D

___ **QUESTION 75:** C

___ **QUESTION 76:** C

___ **QUESTION 77:** A

___ **QUESTION 78:** A

___ **QUESTION 79:** C

___ **QUESTION 80:** C

___ **QUESTION 81:** A

___ **QUESTION 82:** A

___ **QUESTION 83:** B

___ **QUESTION 84:** A

___ **QUESTION 85:** B

___ **QUESTION 86:** B

___ **QUESTION 87:** C

___ **QUESTION 88:** B

___ **QUESTION 89:** D

___ **QUESTION 90:** D

___ **QUESTION 91:** B

___ **QUESTION 92:** C

___ **QUESTION 93:** C

___ **QUESTION 94:** A

___ **QUESTION 95:** D

___ **QUESTION 96:** A

___ **QUESTION 97:** C

___ **QUESTION 98:** D

___ **QUESTION 99:** D

___ **QUESTION 100:** A

___ **QUESTION 101:** A

___ **QUESTION 102:** B

___ **QUESTION 103:** A

___ **QUESTION 104:** A

___ **QUESTION 105:** D

___ **QUESTION 106:** A

___ **QUESTION 107:** B

___ **QUESTION 108:** D

___ **QUESTION 109:** C

___ **QUESTION 110:** B

___ **QUESTION 111:** D

___ **QUESTION 112:** C

___ **QUESTION 113:** B

___ **QUESTION 114:** D

___ **QUESTION 115:** C

___ **QUESTION 116:** A

___ **QUESTION 117:** B

___ **QUESTION 118:** A

___ **QUESTION 119:** D

___ **QUESTION 120:** C

___ **QUESTION 121:** C

___ **QUESTION 122:** A

___ **QUESTION 123:** B

___ **QUESTION 124:** D

___ **QUESTION 125:** D

___ **QUESTION 126:** D

___ **QUESTION 127:** C

___ **QUESTION 128:** B

___ **QUESTION 129:** A

___ **QUESTION 130:** C

___ **QUESTION 131:** C

___ **QUESTION 132:** C

___ **QUESTION 133:** D

___ **QUESTION 134:** C

___ **QUESTION 135:** C

___ **QUESTION 136:** A

___ **QUESTION 137:** C

___ **QUESTION 138:** D

___ **QUESTION 139:** A

___ **QUESTION 140:** B

___ **QUESTION 141:** C

___ **QUESTION 142:** D

___ **QUESTION 143:** D

___ **QUESTION 144:** D

___ **QUESTION 145:** A

___ **QUESTION 146:** A

___ **QUESTION 147:** D

___ **QUESTION 148:** B

___ **QUESTION 149:** C

___ QUESTION 150: B

___ QUESTION 151: B

___ QUESTION 152: D

___ QUESTION 153: C

___ QUESTION 154: A

___ QUESTION 155: D

___ QUESTION 156: C

___ QUESTION 157: C

___ QUESTION 158: A

___ QUESTION 159: D

___ QUESTION 160: B

___ QUESTION 161: B

___ QUESTION 162: A

___ QUESTION 163: C

___ QUESTION 164: A

___ QUESTION 165: C

___ QUESTION 166: D

___ QUESTION 167: D

___ QUESTION 168: C

___ **QUESTION 169:** D

___ **QUESTION 170:** B

___ **QUESTION 171:** C

___ **QUESTION 172:** A

___ **QUESTION 173:** C

___ **QUESTION 174:** B

___ **QUESTION 175:** A

___ **QUESTION 176:** D

___ **QUESTION 177:** B

___ **QUESTION 178:** B

___ **QUESTION 179:** A

___ **QUESTION 180:** B

___ **QUESTION 181:** D

___ **QUESTION 182:** C

___ **QUESTION 183:** C

___ **QUESTION 184:** B

___ **QUESTION 185:** A

___ **QUESTION 186:** D

___ **QUESTION 187:** B

___ QUESTION 188: D

___ QUESTION 189: B

___ QUESTION 190: C

___ QUESTION 191: A

___ QUESTION 192: B

___ QUESTION 193: D

___ QUESTION 194: A

___ QUESTION 195: B

___ QUESTION 196: D

___ QUESTION 197: C

___ QUESTION 198: B

___ QUESTION 199: A

___ QUESTION 200: C

Got your total? Here's how your score breaks down:

YOU'RE OFFICIALLY THE AGGIES STARTING **QB**	= 180 – 200
YOU'RE THE AGGIES FEATURED **RB**	= 160 – 179
YOU'RE THE AGGIES PRIMARY **WR**	= 140 – 159
YOU'RE THE BACK-UP TO THE **RB** WHO BLOCKS	= 120 – 139
I CAN GIVE YOU DIRECTIONS TO COLLEGE STATION	= 119 OR LESS

Think you can do better? Be on the lookout for *Texas A&M Aggies Trivia IQ, Volume II.*

About the Author

BORN AND RAISED in Dallas, TX, Walter B. Littlejohn has a BBA Degree from Texas A&M University and a MS from the University of Texas at Dallas. After graduation from Texas A&M he entered the United States Air Force and graduated from pilot training in 1954. His first assignment as an operational pilot was as an F-89 Scorpion pilot with the 65th Fighter Interceptor Sq. at Elmendorf AFB, Alaska. Future assignments took him to New Mexico, Utah, and Texas and overseas assignments in Japan, Korea, Okinawa and Vietnam, flying the F-86, F-94 and B-57. Included in his various flying assignments, Col. Littlejohn was the command IP (instructor pilot) and Flight Examiner for The Pacific Air Command and Air Defense Command. During his 1967-1968 Vietnam tour, Col. Littlejohn flew 165 combat missions in the B-57 Canberra and was awarded The Distinguished Flying Cross and The Air Medal with eight clusters. When he retired from the Air Force he was serving as Chief of the Air Defense Exercise Branch at Air Defense Command Headquarters in Colorado Springs. After retiring from the Air Force he returned with his family to Texas, where he now resides.

References

- *2010 Texas A&M Media guide – aggieathletics.com*
- *2011 Texas A&M Media guide – aggieathletic.com*
- *espn.com*
- *cbssports.com*
- *tamuscout.com*
- *aggiesports.com*
- *big12sports.com*

About Black Mesa

BLACK MESA IS a Florida-based publishing company that specializes in sports history and trivia books. Look for these popular titles in our trivia IQ series:

- *Mixed Martial Arts (Volumes I & II)*
- *Boston Red Sox (Volumes I & II)*
- *Tampa Bay Rays*
- *New York Yankees*
- *Atlanta Braves*
- *Major League Baseball*
- *Milwaukee Brewers*
- *St. Louis Cardinals*
- *Boston Celtics*
- *University of Florida Gators Football*
- *University of Georgia Bulldogs Football*
- *University of Texas Longhorns Football*
- *New England Patriots*

For information about special discounts for bulk purchases, please email:

black.mesa.publishing@gmail.com

www.blackmesabooks.com

Sports by the Numbers Series

- *Major League Baseball*
- *New York Yankees*
- *Boston Red Sox*
- *San Francisco Giants*
- *University of Oklahoma Football*
- *University of Georgia Football*
- *Penn State University Football*
- *NASCAR*
- *Sacramento Kings Basketball*
- *Mixed Martial Arts*

Available Soon

- *Texas Rangers*
- *Los Angeles Dodgers*
- *Boston Celtics*
- *Dallas Cowboys*